D0842945

WHY DO SOME PEOPLE WEAR GLASSES?

BY ISAAC ASIMOV AND CARRIE DIERKS

Gareth Stevens Publishing
MILWAUKEE

For a free color catalog describing Gareth Stevens's list of high-quality children's books, call 1-800-341-3569 (USA) or 1-800-461-9120 (Canada).

The editor would like to thank Martha F. Jay, Ph.D., M.D., of Mequon, Wisconsin, for her assistance with the accuracy of the text and artwork.

Library of Congress Cataloging-in-Publication Data

Asimov, Isaac, 1920-
  Why do some people wear glasses? / by Isaac Asimov and Carrie
Dierks.
      p. cm. -- (Ask Isaac Asimov)
  Includes bibliographical references and index.
  Summary: Briefly describes how our eyes work, various vision
problems, and how glasses can help us see better.
  ISBN 0-8368-0809-6
  1. Eyeglasses--Juvenile literature. 2. Vision--Juvenile
literature. 3. Vision disorders--Juvenile literature. [1. Vision.
2. Eyeglasses.] I. Dierks, Carrie. II. Title. III. Series:
Asimov, Isaac, 1920-   Ask Isaac Asimov.
RE976.A83 1993
617.7'522--dc20   93-20156

Edited, designed, and produced by
Gareth Stevens Publishing
1555 North RiverCenter Drive, Suite 201
Milwaukee, Wisconsin 53212, USA

Picture Credits
pp. 2-3, Marilyn Hamann and Joan Knuteson/Advertising Art Studios, 1993; pp. 4-5, © Barry Clothier/Adams Picture Library; pp. 6-7, Kurt Carloni/Artisan, 1993; pp. 8-9, Paul Miller/Advertising Art Studios, 1993; p. 9 (inset), Paul Miller/Advertising Art Studios, 1993; p. 10, © John Adams/Adams Picture Library; p. 11, © John Adams/ Adams Picture Library; pp. 12-13, Marilyn Hamann and Joan Knuteson/Advertising Art Studios, 1993; p. 12 (inset), Paul Miller/Advertising Art Studios, 1993; pp. 14-15, Courtesy of American Academy of Ophthalmology; p. 14 (inset), © SIU/Visuals Unlimited; pp. 16-17, Paul Miller/Advertising Art Studios, 1993; pp. 18-19, Christiane Schreiner, 1993; p. 18 (inset), © Camerique/H. Armstrong Roberts; pp. 20-21, © Richard Gardner/Barnaby's Picture Library; pp. 22-23, © Camerique/H. Armstrong Roberts; p. 24, Paul Miller/Advertising Art Studios, 1993

Cover photograph, © Garth Roberts/Adams Picture Library: A lovely Japanese girl is proud to be wearing her glasses.

Series editor: Barbara J. Behm
Series designer: Sabine Beaupré
Book designer: Kristi Ludwig
Art coordinator: Karen Knutson
Picture researcher: Diane Laska

Printed in the United States of America

1 2 3 4 5 6 7 8 9 98 97 96 95 94 93

Contents

Words that appear in the glossary are printed in **boldface** type the first time they occur in the text.

Learning about Your Body

Think about all the wonderful things your body can do. Most people usually feel strong and healthy and can carry out the day's activities without even thinking. But all the parts of the human body don't always work perfectly.

For example, some people don't see as well as others. These people must wear eyeglasses to improve their eyesight. Why do some people have poor eyesight? How do glasses help people see better? Let's find out.

4

A Look at Your Eyes

Thousands of times a day, your eyes focus on images, or pictures, of the world around you. These images then travel to your brain, which "tells" you what you see.

Images are formed from rays of light. Light passes through the clear, protective **cornea** of your eye to the part of your eye called the **pupil**. The pupil is the round, black opening in the middle of your eye. The colored part of the eye, called the **iris**, controls the size of the pupil. It lets in the necessary amount of light for clear vision.

6

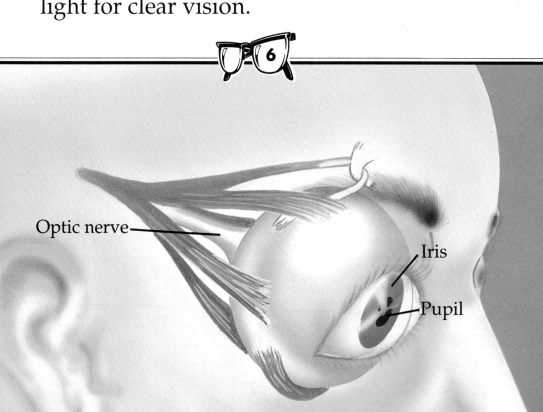

Optic nerve

Iris

Pupil

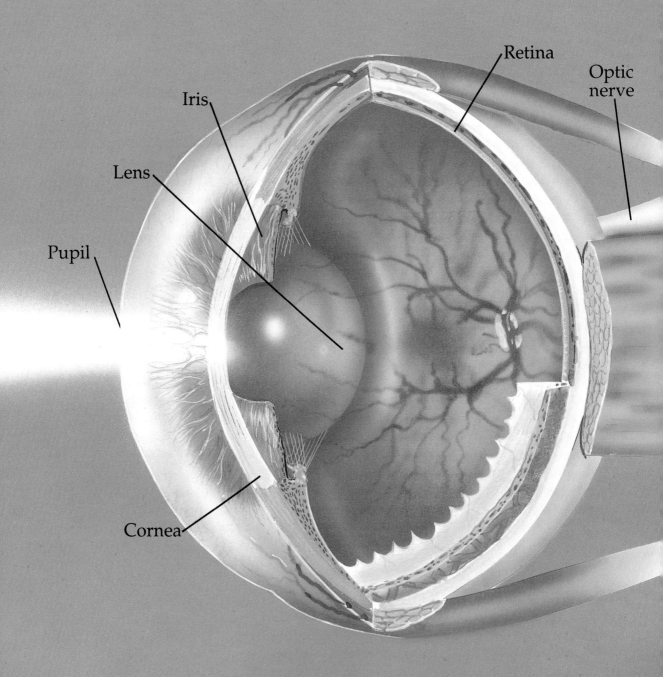

Retina

Optic nerve

Iris

Lens

Pupil

Cornea

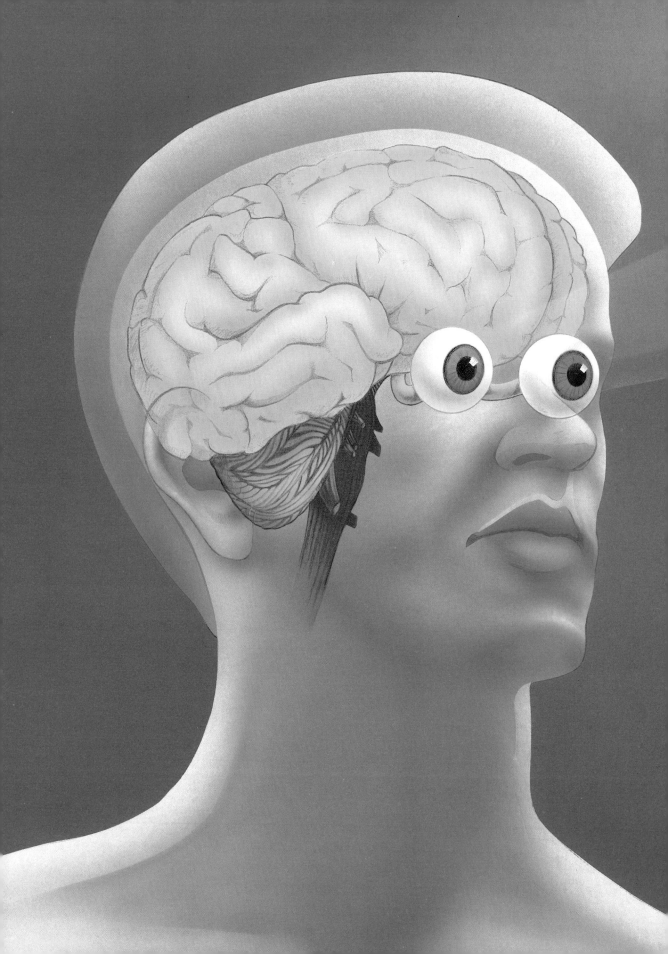

Seeing the Light

Behind the iris is the **lens**. The lens can become thicker or thinner to bend and focus the light rays. From the lens, the light rays are projected onto the **retina** at the back of the eye. At this point, the images appear upside down on the retina. The retina acts like the film in a camera. It turns the light into electrical impulses that travel along the **optic nerve** to the brain. Your brain interprets these impulses. It turns the image right side up and allows you to "see" color, shape, movement, and distance.

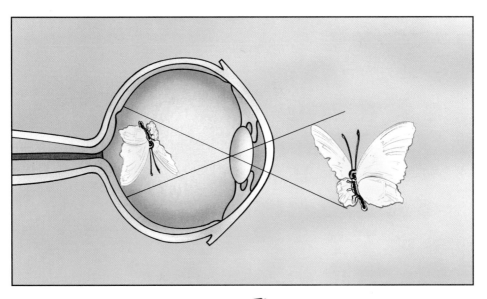

In and Out of Focus

When your eyes are working just right, you see objects in clear focus. But, for some people, objects look blurry. People whose eyes cannot focus clearly are said to have either **myopia** or **hyperopia**. Myopia, sometimes called nearsightedness, occurs when the eye is too long so the image comes into focus in front of the retina. With hyperopia, which is sometimes called

10

farsightedness, the opposite is true. These people have an eye that is too short so the image comes into focus behind the retina. Eyeglasses can correct both of these problems. Many people also have trouble seeing vertical, horizontal, or diagonal lines. This condition is called **astigmatism**. It is caused by an irregularly shaped cornea and can also be corrected by eyeglasses.

11

Another Pair of Eyes

How do eyeglasses work? They work like the lenses of your eyes! The main difference is that eyeglass lenses bend light rays before the rays reach your eyes. This focuses the image properly, allowing you to see objects clearly.

A **convex** lens bends rays of light inward to correct hyperopia, or farsightedness. A **concave** lens spreads rays of light to correct myopia, or nearsightedness.

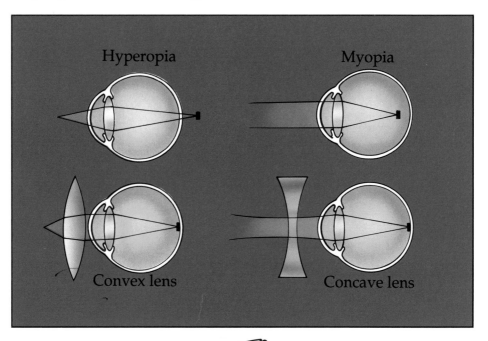

Do I Need Glasses?

Your eye doctor will test your vision by having you read a chart that contains rows of letters. If you can read every letter from 20 feet (about 6 meters) away, you have perfect, or what is called 20/20, vision. If you have trouble reading some letters, the doctor will have you look through different lenses to find the ones that improve your vision. Then the appropriate eyeglass lenses will be made for you.

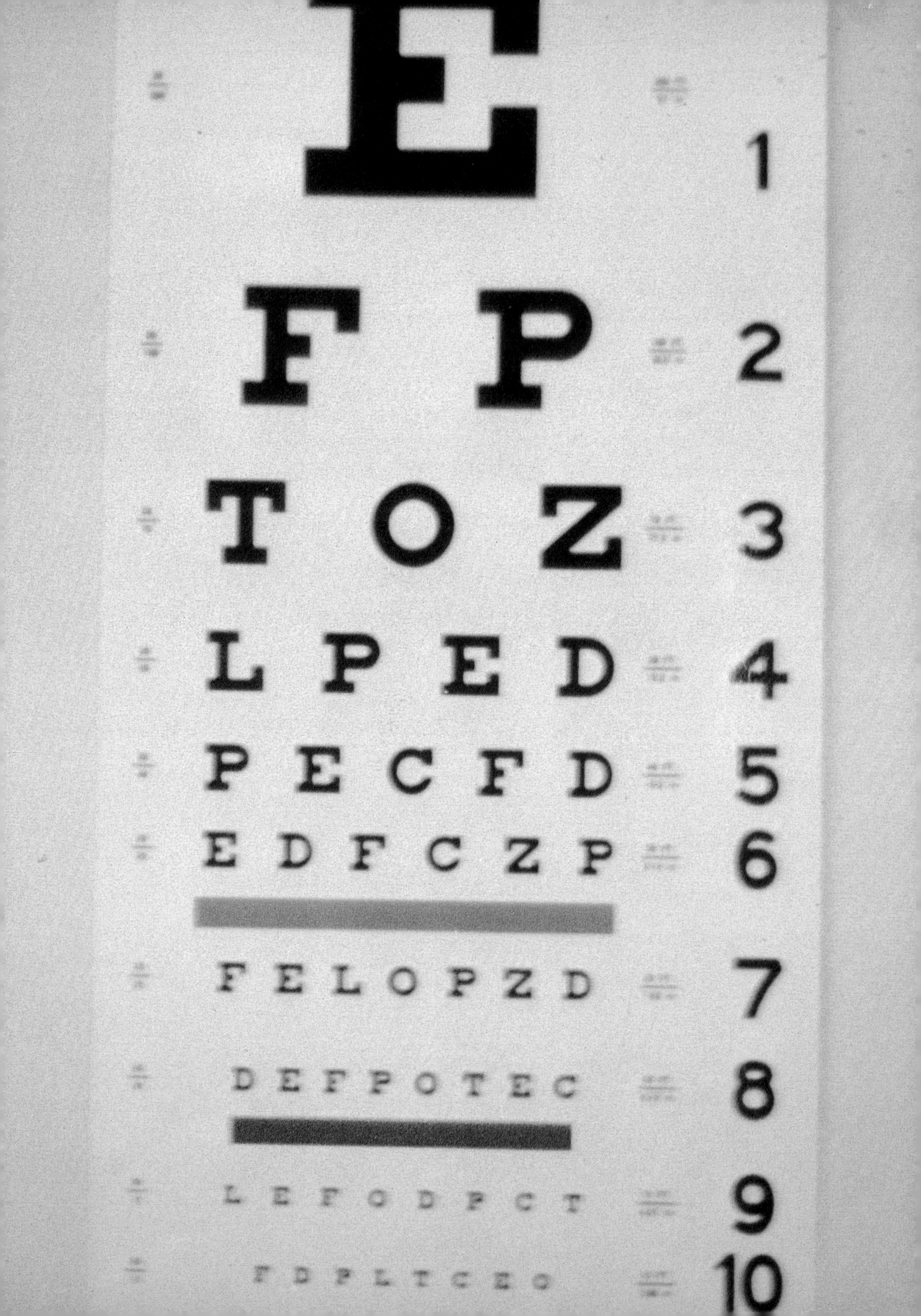

E

1

F P

2

T O Z

3

L P E D

4

P E C F D

5

E D F C Z P

6

F E L O P Z D

7

D E F P O T E C

8

L E F O D P C T

9

F D P L T C E O

10

Other Kinds of Lenses

Glasses don't just correct blurry vision. They also correct double vision or help you see in the dark. Some glasses, called **bifocals**, are like two pairs in one. One part of the glasses helps you see distant objects. Another part helps you see objects that are near.

16

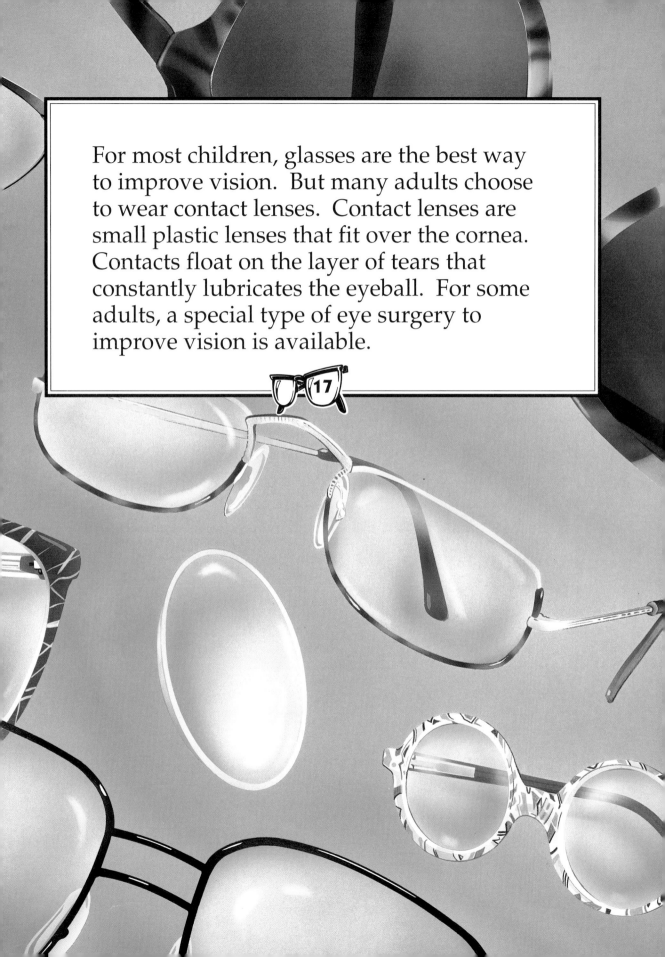

For most children, glasses are the best way to improve vision. But many adults choose to wear contact lenses. Contact lenses are small plastic lenses that fit over the cornea. Contacts float on the layer of tears that constantly lubricates the eyeball. For some adults, a special type of eye surgery to improve vision is available.

17

Living with Blindness

Some eye problems are so severe that wearing glasses doesn't help. A birth defect, a disease, or an accident may leave a person unable to see at all. People who are blind must rely on hearing and touch to learn about the world. They listen to books on tape and read **braille**, a special alphabet of raised dots. They use guide dogs or canes to help them get from place to place. With the help of tools like these, blind people are able to lead full lives.

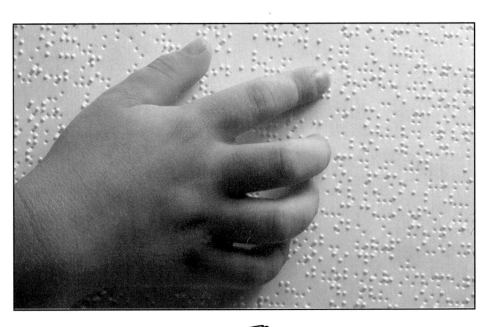

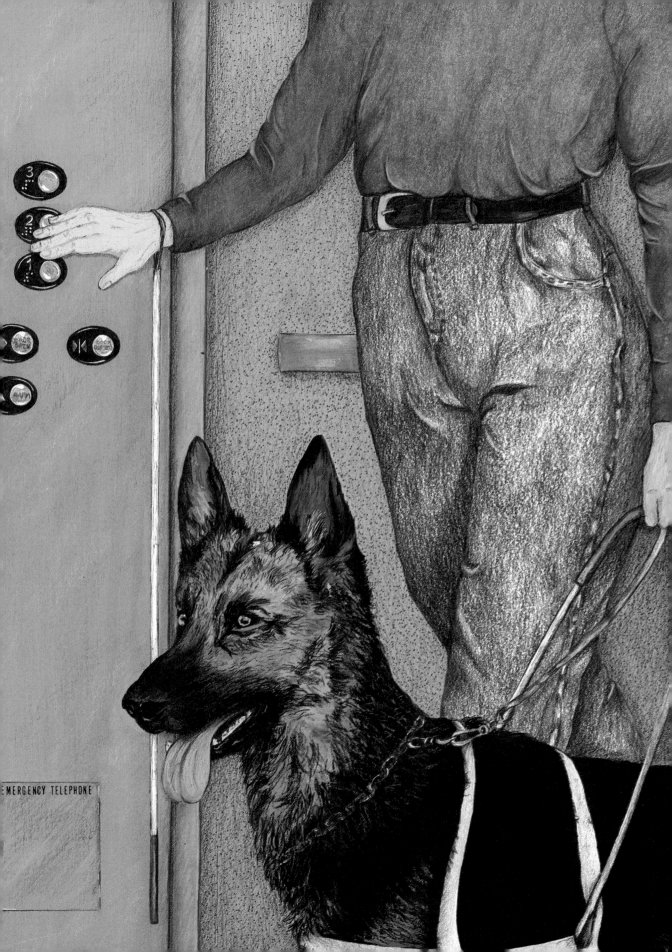

Don't Ruin Your Eyes!

People have many different beliefs about what is good or bad for the eyes. But are all these beliefs correct? For instance, does eating carrots make you see better? No, but carrots do contain vitamins that keep your eyes healthy. What about reading in dim

20

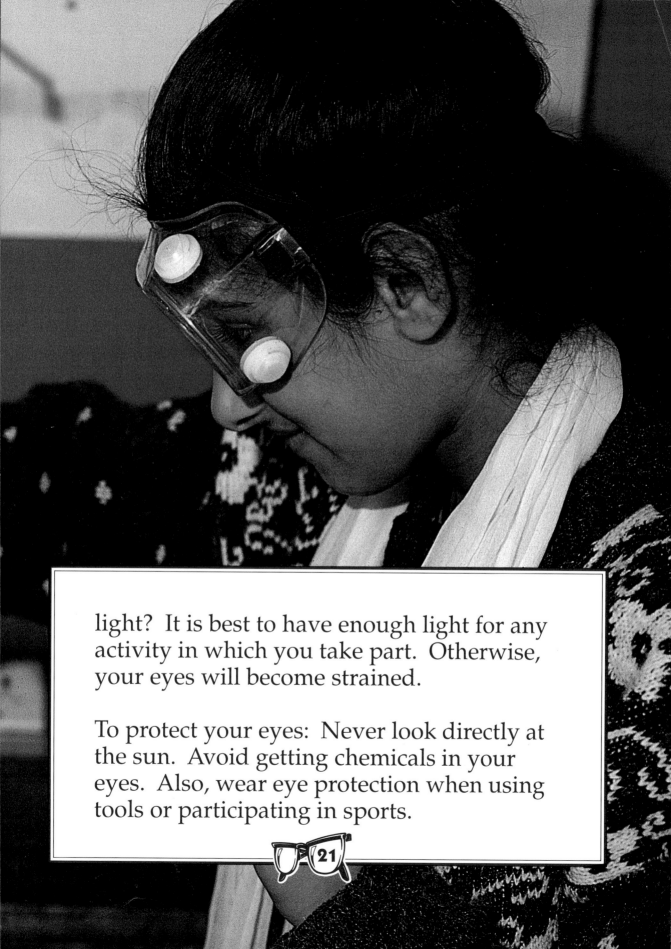

light? It is best to have enough light for any activity in which you take part. Otherwise, your eyes will become strained.

To protect your eyes: Never look directly at the sun. Avoid getting chemicals in your eyes. Also, wear eye protection when using tools or participating in sports.

21

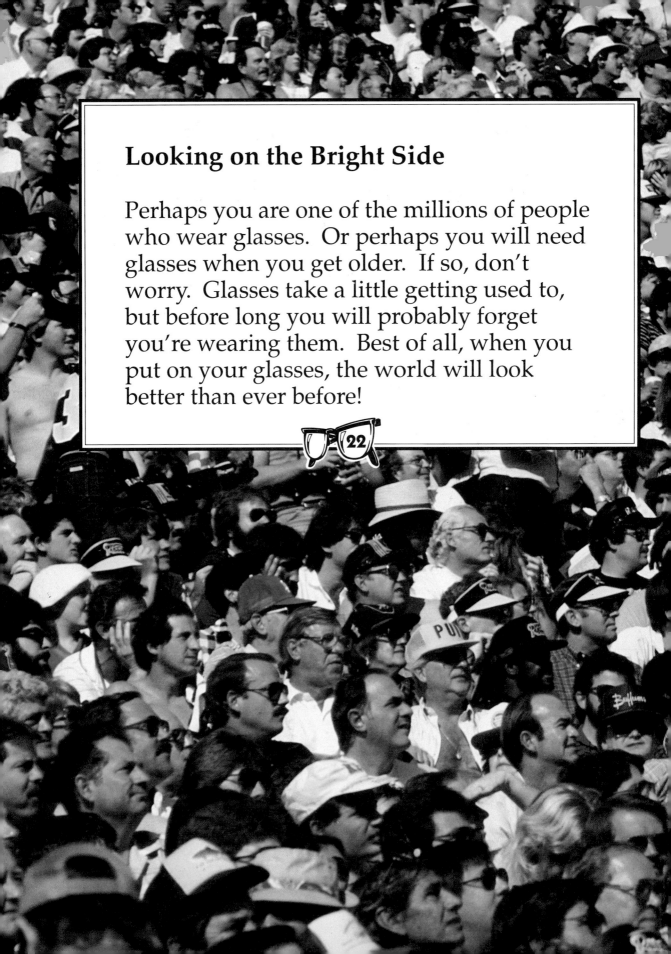

Looking on the Bright Side

Perhaps you are one of the millions of people who wear glasses. Or perhaps you will need glasses when you get older. If so, don't worry. Glasses take a little getting used to, but before long you will probably forget you're wearing them. Best of all, when you put on your glasses, the world will look better than ever before!

22

More Books to Read

Seeing by Kathie Billingslea Smith and Victoria Crenson
(Troll Associates)
Seeing in Special Ways — Children Living with Blindness by Thomas
Bergman (Gareth Stevens)
Sight, Light, and Color Science Universe Series (Arco Publishers)

Places to Write

Here are some places you can write for more information about
eyesight. Be sure to tell them exactly what you want to know. Give
them your full name and address so they can write back to you.

American Academy of
Ophthalmology
P.O. Box 7424
San Francisco, CA 94120-7424

Canadian Association
of Optometrists
#301, 1785 Alta Vista Dr.
Ottawa, Ontario K1G 3Y6

Glossary

astigmatism (uh-STIG-muh-tism): a condition in which a person
has difficulty focusing on horizontal, vertical, or diagonal
lines. It is caused by an irregularly shaped cornea.

bifocals (BYE-fo-calz): a double eyeglass lens in which the top
portion helps a person see distant objects and the bottom
portion helps a person see objects that are nearby.

braille (brayle): an alphabet used by blind people in which each
letter of the normal alphabet corresponds to a pattern of raised
dots. It was developed by Louis Braille in 1829.

concave (kon-CAVE): curving inward.

convex (kon-VEKS): curving outward.

cornea (CORN-ee-uh): the clear, protective covering over the eye.

hyperopia (high-per-OPE-ih-ah): having an eye that is too short so that images focus behind the retina (also called farsightedness).

iris (EYE-riss): the colored portion of the eye that controls the size of the pupil.

lens (lenz): the part of the eye that bends and focuses light rays.

myopia (my-OPE-ih-ah): having an eye that is too long so that images focus in front of the retina (also called nearsightedness).

optic nerve (OP-tick): the nerve that carries impulses from the eye to the brain.

pupil (PUPE-ill): the opening in the center of the eye that lets in light.

retina (RET-ih-nuh): the back of the eye that is sensitive to light. The retina converts light images to impulses that are, in turn, sent to the brain.

Index